ASTRONOMY

CONTENTS

THE MAGNIFICENT HEAVENS

THE night sky is one of the great delights of nature. There is always something fascinating to see there. The stars wheel overhead as the night goes by, bright planets stand out like beacons, meteors burn up and leave fiery trails, the Moon waxes and wanes, comets suddenly appear and just as suddenly disappear. It is no wonder that people down the ages have studied the starry skies – the heavens – closely. Studying the heavens is a science we call astronomy. Using their eyes, telescopes, satellites and other equipment, astronomers have built up a clear picture of what our universe is like.

Part of a star map dating from the early 1700s, showing fanciful figures for the star patterns (constellations).

Star positions
This is an ancient astronomical instrument called an astrolabe. Early astronomers used astrolabes to observe the positions of heavenly bodies.

Ancient monuments

About 4,000 years ago, the Ancient Egyptians built their pyramids (*above*) to line up with certain stars. At about the same time, the Ancient Britons started to build Stonehenge (*below*), near Salisbury, as a kind of astronomical observatory.

Space travel

Astronomers now use space satellites to study the heavenly bodies. These spacecraft carry telescopes and other instruments into space. There, they can view the heavens more clearly.

Modern observatories

Astronomers work at observatories, such as Palomar in California, USA (*right*). The dome houses a large telescope, which gathers the faint light the stars give out.

GETTING STARTED

STARGAZING is a great hobby, and you do not need a lot of expensive equipment for it. Just go outside on a clear, dark night and look up at the sky. The starry heavens look great no matter where you happen to live in the world. However, you will enjoy an evening's stargazing more if you spend a little time preparing for it beforehand. The main thing you need to do is to make sure you are warm, because you will be standing about or sitting for a long time. The best stargazing nights are usually the coldest! This is because they have no clouds, which often act as a blanket to keep the Earth warm. So you will need warm clothes and hot drinks.

The heavens look great just using your eyes. When you look at them through binoculars, they look magnificent.

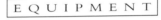

EQUIPMENT

You will need: binoculars, bag, gloves, scarf, warm headgear, flask with hot drink, snack.

Get comfortable

You need to be as comfortable as possible when you go stargazing. In the garden, a deckchair is ideal. If you venture farther afield, a camping stool is easier to carry. And remember your star map!

7

EQUIPMENT

You will need: broom handles, sticky tape, twine, scissors, binoculars.

Mount your binoculars

You will enjoy stargazing more when you use binoculars. The trouble is, good binoculars are quite heavy, and holding them up to your eyes for more than a few minutes is tiring. So it is a good idea to make a simple tripod to mount them on.

Support your binoculars

To make the tripod, tape the top ends of three broom handles together. Then spread the bottom ends out in a triangular shape until the top is at the right height for your eyes. Tie bits of twine between them to help stop the legs splaying apart. When you have made your tripod, mount your binoculars on top. Tie them in position with the twine. Make sure that the focusing ring on top of the binoculars is free to move.

A planisphere is a useful aid to stargazing. It shows you which stars to look out for in the sky at any time of the year.

PATTERNS IN THE SKY

THE night sky is full of stars. If you counted them, you would find that you could see several thousand at any time with the naked eye. But not all stars are the same. Some are much brighter than others. The bright stars form patterns in the sky.

If you are a keen stargazer, you can quickly learn to recognize the star patterns and they will help you to find your way through the night sky. We call these star patterns the constellations. They change little year after year. Over 2,000 years ago, the astronomers of Ancient Greece saw much the same constellations as we do. They gave the constellations the names we use today. They named them after the people, animals and objects they thought the patterns looked like. They also made up stories about how these figures got into the heavens.

Taurus, the Bull

Leo, the Lion
The pattern of stars in the constellation Leo do look quite like the front part of a crouching lion.

Ancient astronomers pictured Orion as a mighty hunter (below).

Find Orion
Orion is one of the easiest constellations to recognize in the night sky *(left)*. It can be seen well in both the northern and the southern hemispheres. The diagram *(right)* shows the pattern made by its brightest stars.

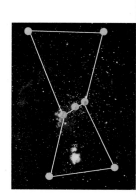

ORION

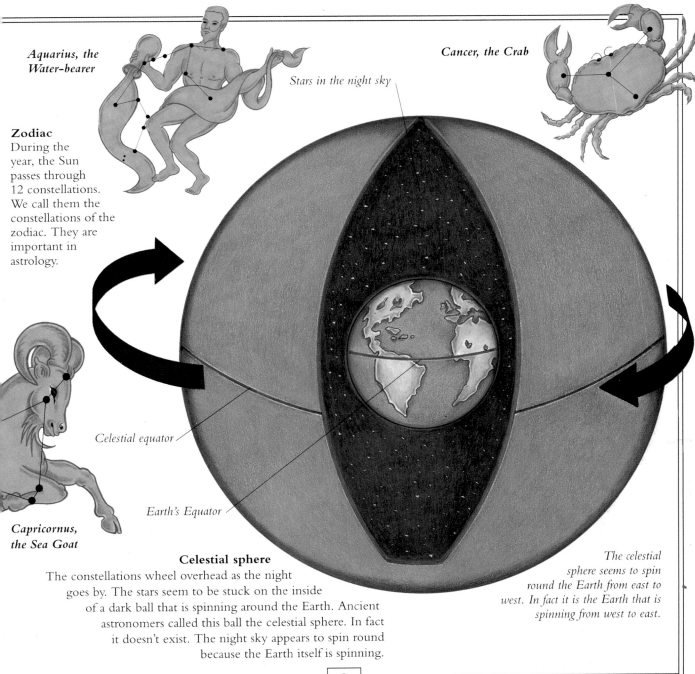

*Aquarius, the
Water-bearer*

Cancer, the Crab

Stars in the night sky

Zodiac
During the
year, the Sun
passes through
12 constellations.
We call them the
constellations of the
zodiac. They are
important in
astrology.

Celestial equator

Earth's Equator

*Capricornus,
the Sea Goat*

Celestial sphere
The constellations wheel overhead as the night
goes by. The stars seem to be stuck on the inside
of a dark ball that is spinning around the Earth. Ancient
astronomers called this ball the celestial sphere. In fact
it doesn't exist. The night sky appears to spin round
because the Earth itself is spinning.

*The celestial
sphere seems to spin
round the Earth from east to
west. In fact it is the Earth that is
spinning from west to east.*

PHOTOGRAPHING THE STARS

You will need: rolls of ordinary film, camera, shutter-release cable, tripod.

YOU can take photographs of the night sky with simple equipment and ordinary film. To photograph the stars, you need a camera with a time-exposure (B setting). This is because the stars do not give out much light, and you have to open the camera shutter for quite a long time before they show up on the film. You also need to mount the camera on a tripod to keep it steady while you have the shutter open. This stops it wobbling and blurring your picture. Use a shutter-release cable for the same reason.

Stars make trails in a picture taken with a camera pointing at the horizon.

Photograph the night sky

1 First, make sure your camera is loaded with film. Screw the shutter-release cable into the camera shutter. Then screw the camera in place on the head of the tripod.

2 Using the "tilt" handle on the tripod, line up the camera with the horizon and tighten the clamp. Make sure that nothing blocks your view!

3 Press the shutter-release cable to open the shutter. Tighten the release in the open position. Leave it for some time, an hour at least, before you close the shutter.

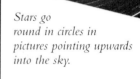

4 Now use the tilt handle again to point the camera upwards at an angle of about 45 degrees. Tighten the clamp and advance the film.

5 Press the shutter-release cable again to open the camera shutter. Tighten the release in the open position. Wait for an hour or so before you close it.

Stars go round in circles in pictures pointing upwards into the sky.

Not really a star
The morning star and the evening star are really a planet, Venus. It got its two names because, at times, it shines quite brightly at dawn and at twilight.

NORTHERN CONSTELLATIONS

Northern celestial hemisphere   *Earth*

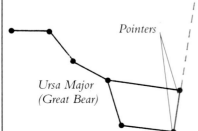

On these pages we talk about constellations of the northern celestial hemisphere.

BECAUSE the Earth is round, you can see only part of the celestial sphere at any time. People in Canada, for example, will not be able to see the constellations that people in New Zealand can see. This is because Canada is in the far northern hemisphere of the world and New Zealand is in the far southern hemisphere. Just as we divide the world into two halves, north and south, so we divide the celestial sphere into two hemispheres. The star map opposite shows the constellations we can see in the northern celestial hemisphere. We often call them the northern constellations.

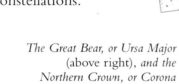

Ursa Minor (Little Bear)

Pole Star

Pointers

Ursa Major (Great Bear)

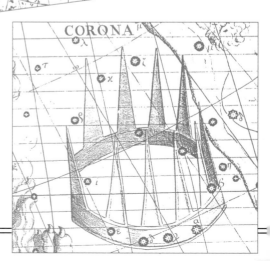

The Great Bear, or Ursa Major (above right), *and the Northern Crown, or Corona Borealis* (right), *as they appear on an old star map.*

Finding stars

The stars in some constellations act as signposts to help us find the stars in other constellations. Two stars in Ursa Major help us find the Pole Star.

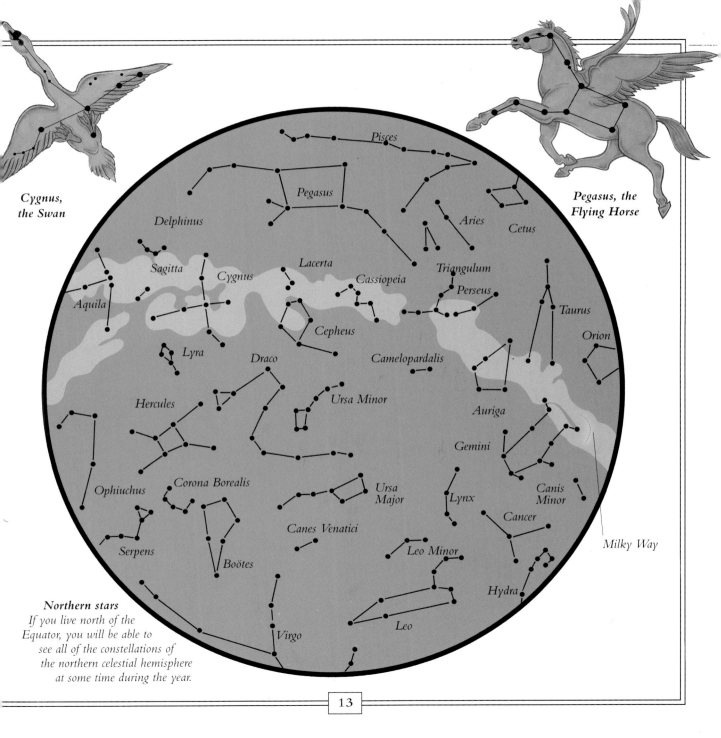

Cygnus,
the Swan

Pegasus, the
Flying Horse

Pisces

Pegasus

Aries

Cetus

Delphinus

Lacerta

Triangulum

Sagitta

Cygnus

Cassiopeia

Perseus

Taurus

Aquila

Cepheus

Orion

Lyra

Draco

Camelopardalis

Hercules

Ursa Minor

Auriga

Gemini

Ophiuchus

Corona Borealis

Ursa
Major

Lynx

Canis
Minor

Cancer

Milky Way

Serpens

Canes Venatici

Leo Minor

Boötes

Hydra

Northern stars

*If you live north of the
Equator, you will be able to
see all of the constellations of
the northern celestial hemisphere
at some time during the year.*

Virgo

Leo

13

SOUTHERN CONSTELLATIONS

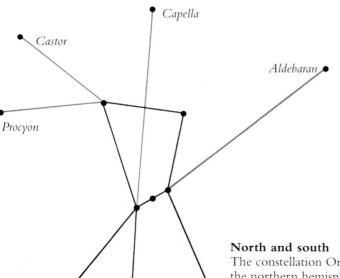

Earth

T
HE map opposite shows constellations of the southern celestial hemisphere. They include such splendid constellations as Scorpius, the Scorpion, and Centaurus, the Centaur. Southern skies are in general more brilliant than northern ones and have the three brightest stars in the heavens – Sirius, Canopus and Alpha Centauri. The northern and southern parts of the celestial sphere meet at what is called the celestial equator. Constellations around the celestial equator can be seen by both northern and southern astronomers at some times of the year.

Southern celestial hemisphere

On these pages we talk about constellations of the southern celestial hemisphere.

Capella

Castor

Aldebaran

Procyon

The constellation Scorpius, the Scorpion, pictured on an ancient star map.

North and south
The constellation Orion lies half in the northern hemisphere and half in the southern. It is a useful signpost to both northern and southern stars.

Sirius

Rigel

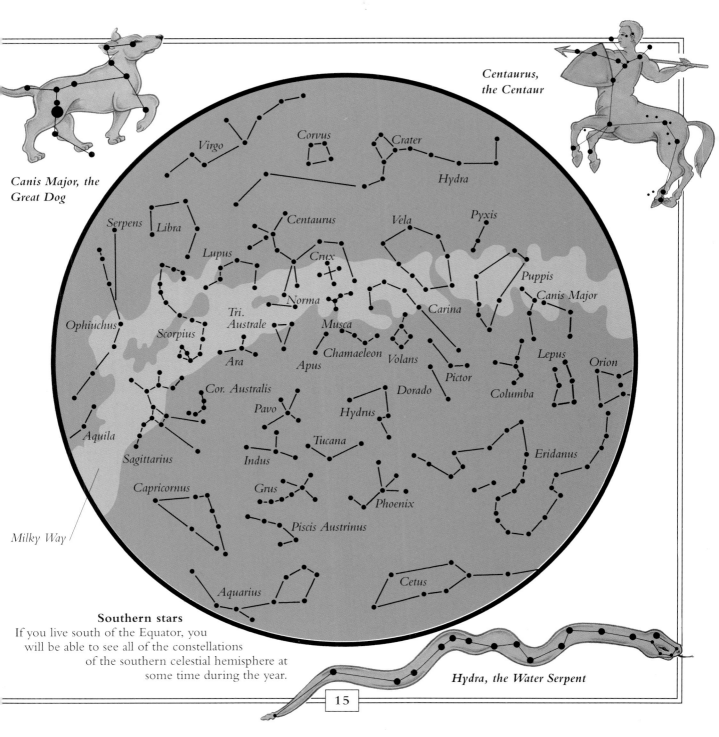

Canis Major, the
Great Dog

Centaurus,
the Centaur

Virgo
Corvus
Crater
Hydra

Serpens
Libra
Centaurus
Vela
Pyxis

Lupus
Crux
Puppis
Canis Major

Ophiuchus
Norma
Carina
Pyxis

Scorpius
Tri.
Australe
Musca
Chamaeleon
Volans
Lepus
Orion

Ara
Apus
Pictor
Columba

Aquila
Cor. Australis
Pavo
Hydrus
Dorado

Sagittarius
Indus
Tucana
Eridanus

Capricornus
Grus
Phoenix

Milky Way
Piscis Austrinus

Aquarius
Cetus

Southern stars
If you live south of the Equator, you
will be able to see all of the constellations
of the southern celestial hemisphere at
some time during the year.

Hydra, the Water Serpent

MAKE A NIGHT SKY

Y OU can become more familiar with the night sky by making pictures of it and putting them on the walls – maybe even the ceiling – of your room. But ask your parents first! Select the part of the night sky you want to show by looking at a star map or a planisphere. Then draw the star patterns (constellations) onto dark blue card. You can also add some of the other things that you might see in the heavens, such as comets and meteors. Use fluorescent materials if possible, so you can see the heavenly bodies shine in your night sky.

M A T E R I A L S

You will need: dark blue card, fluorescent stars and dots, fluorescent paints, paintbrushes.

Use a planisphere to choose the star patterns you want to copy.

Make a star map

1 Copy the star patterns from a star map onto the dark blue card. Make up your own shapes to link the stars if you want to.

2 Stick dots in place in the star patterns. You can use different coloured dots where you want to. Real stars have different colours.

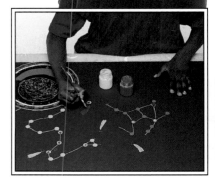

3 When you have finished your star patterns, add objects such as comets. Use stars for their heads, and paint in their tails.

Stars in 3D

From the Earth, it looks as if the stars are stuck on the inside of a huge upturned bowl. They all seem to be the same distance away, and they do not seem to move about. In fact, the stars are all at different distances away from us, and they do move about. We cannot see them move because they are too far away. This mobile will give you an idea of how the stars are arranged in space.

Make a mobile

1 Make three circles with the wire. Wind the wire around the bowl to get the right size and shape. Tie or tape the wire circles together to form a ball shape.

2 Paint the table tennis balls with the fluorescent paint – use lots of colours. Tie (or glue) a different length of thread to each.

3 Tie the painted table tennis balls to the wire circles. Then hang the whole thing from the ceiling. Your mobile shows how the stars are scattered about in space, all at different distances from us. Spin it and you will see the stars move.

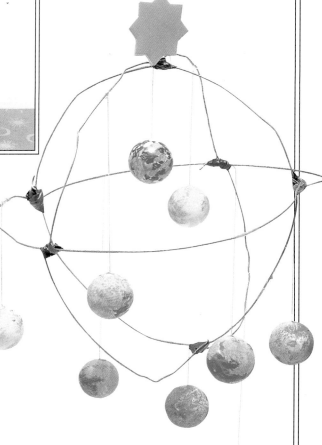

SEASONAL STARS

Earth in June
One half of the celestial sphere
Earth's orbit
Sun
Other half of celestial sphere
Earth in December

W̲E see different constellations in the night sky season by season. This is because at different times of the year we look at different parts of the celestial sphere. If you live in the northern hemisphere, you will see the greatest changes in the night sky when you look south. Different constellations appear in the sky in the summer and in the winter. If you live in the southern hemisphere, you will see the greatest changes in the sky when you look north. The maps opposite show how the constellations change between summer and winter in the southern hemisphere.

Round the Sun
The Earth circles around the Sun once a year. At any time, we can see only one-half of the celestial sphere. We cannot see the other half because the Sun blots it out. Six months later we can see the other half, while the Sun blocks out the first half.

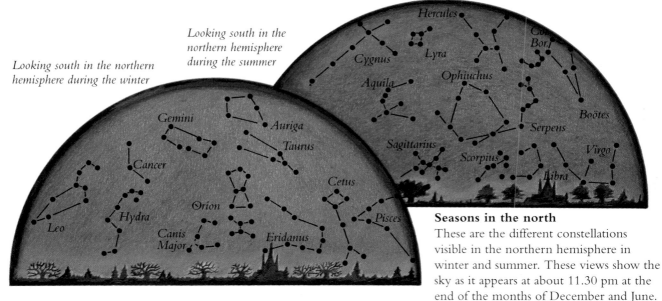

Looking south in the northern hemisphere during the summer

Looking south in the northern hemisphere during the winter

Hercules
Cygnus
Lyra
Co. Bor.
Aquila
Ophiuchus
Sagittarius
Serpeus
Boötes
Scorpius
Virgo
Libra

Gemini
Auriga
Taurus
Cancer
Cetus
Leo
Hydra
Orion
Pisces
Canis Major
Eridanus

Seasons in the north
These are the different constellations visible in the northern hemisphere in winter and summer. These views show the sky as it appears at about 11.30 pm at the end of the months of December and June.

A cloud of dust appears among the stars in the constellation Cygnus, the Swan. It looks like a shimmering veil, and is called the Veil Nebula.

A region of the Milky Way in the southern hemisphere. You can see this fuzzy band in the night sky when it is really dark.

Looking north in the southern hemisphere during the winter

Looking north in the southern hemisphere during the summer

Seasons in the south

These are the different constellations visible in the southern hemisphere in winter and summer. These views show the sky as it appears at about 11.30 pm at the end of the months of June and December.

USING A PLANISPHERE

A planisphere will help you to find your way around the heavens. It consists of two discs held together in the centre. The top one has a window, and a scale marked with the time of the day and night. The bottom one carries a star map, and has a scale marked in days of the year. When you move the discs to line up the time and day you want to stargaze, the stars to look out for appear in the window. Different stars can be seen from different parts of the world, or latitudes. So, there are different planispheres for different latitudes.

Three planispheres for different latitudes.

You will need: planisphere, watch or clock, compass.

Finding stars

1 Let us say you want to go stargazing on 15 September. Get out your planisphere and check the time. Say it is 11 pm.

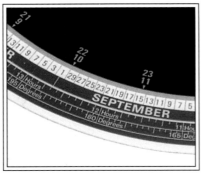

2 Suppose you live in the northern hemisphere at about latitude 42 degrees north. Turn the discs until 11 on the top one lines up with 15 September on the bottom one. The stars visible at this time now appear in the window.

3 Suppose you live in the southern hemisphere at about latitude 35 degrees south. Turn the discs until 11 on the top one lines up with 15 September on the bottom one. The stars visible at this time now appear in the window.

North or south?

If you live in the northern hemisphere, hold the planisphere above your head, face down, so that "midnight" on the top scale points north. The planisphere is now in the right position. If you live in the southern hemisphere, hold the planisphere so that "midnight" on the top scale points south. The planisphere is now in the right position.

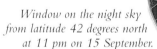

Window on the night sky from latitude 42 degrees north at 11 pm on 15 September.

4 Now you have to check with a compass which direction is north and which is south. This helps you position your planisphere properly so that the window shows the sky the right way up.

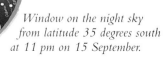

Window on the night sky from latitude 35 degrees south at 11 pm on 15 September.

WHAT STARS ARE LIKE

To our eyes, the stars are tiny pinpoints of light. But in fact they are really big. They are bodies like our Sun, made up of hot glowing gas. Like the Sun, they give off energy as light, heat and other forms of radiation. The reason stars appear to be so tiny is because they are so far away. Even nearby stars are over 40 million million kilometres away. It takes a beam of light from these stars over four years to reach us. So astronomers say that these stars lie over four light-years away. They use the "light-year" as a unit to measure distances to the stars.

Some of the bright stars in the constellation Perseus.

Space travel
Imagine you could ride in a starship that could travel at the speed of light. This speed is 300,000 kilometres per second. It would take you just eight and a half minutes to travel to the Sun. It would take you more than four years to reach even the next nearest star!

Starship

Earth

Bright and dim
In the night sky, we can see that some stars look brighter than others. But a star that looks bright may not really be brighter than a star that looks dim. The star that looks dim might be a truly bright star that is a long, long way off. The star that looks bright might be a truly dim star that is quite close to us.

The nearest star to the Sun is a small faint red star called Proxima Centauri.

Nearest star

Star sizes

Stars come in all sizes. Our local star, the Sun, has a diameter of about 1,400,000 kilometres. This is more than 100 times bigger than the Earth's diameter. But compared with many other stars, the Sun is tiny, as the picture shows. Astronomers call it a dwarf star. Stars called red giants are very much bigger, and ones called supergiants are unbelievably big. Supergiants can measure hundreds of millions of kilometres across.

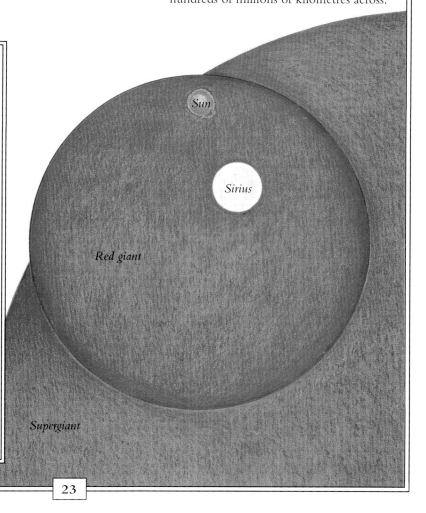

Sun

Sirius

Red giant

Supergiant

BRIGHTEST STARS

Star	Constellation	Magnitude★
Sirius	Canis Major	-1.4
Canopus	Carina	-0.7
Alpha Centauri	Centaurus	-0.2
Arcturus	Boötes	-0.1
Vega	Lyra	0.0
Capella	Auriga	0.1

★ We measure the brightness of a star on a scale of magnitude. The brightest stars we see are of magnitude 1 or below. The faintest ones are of magnitude 6.

NEAREST STARS

Star	Constellation	Distance★ (light-years)
Prox. Centauri	Centaurus	4.3
Alpha Centauri	Centaurus	4.3
Bernard's star	Ophiuchus	5.8
Wolf 359	Leo	7.6
Lalande 21185	Ursa Major	8.1
Sirius	Canis Major	8.7

★ 1 light-year is the distance light travels in a year, nearly 10 million million kilometres.

CLUSTERS AND CLOUDS

MANY stars travel through space in groups. Some travel in twos and threes, but others travel in groups of hundreds and even thousands. We call these large groups of stars "clusters". In many groups, the stars are quite far apart, and we call them open clusters. But in other groups, the stars are packed closely together to form great balls (globes). We call them globular clusters.

Clusters are found dotted about among the constellations. So are objects we call nebulae (singular, nebula). The word "nebula" means "cloud". Nebulae are great clouds of gas and dust. Bright nebulae are lit up by nearby stars. Dark nebulae can be seen only when they block the light from stars behind them.

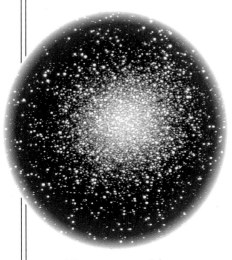

This great mass of stars is a globular cluster. It contains hundreds of thousands of stars packed closely together.

The Ring Nebula looks rather like a smoke ring. It is a ring of gas puffed out by a star in the centre.

This nebula is called the Tarantula, because it looks rather like the large hairy spider of that name. It is found in a galaxy called the Large Magellanic Cloud.

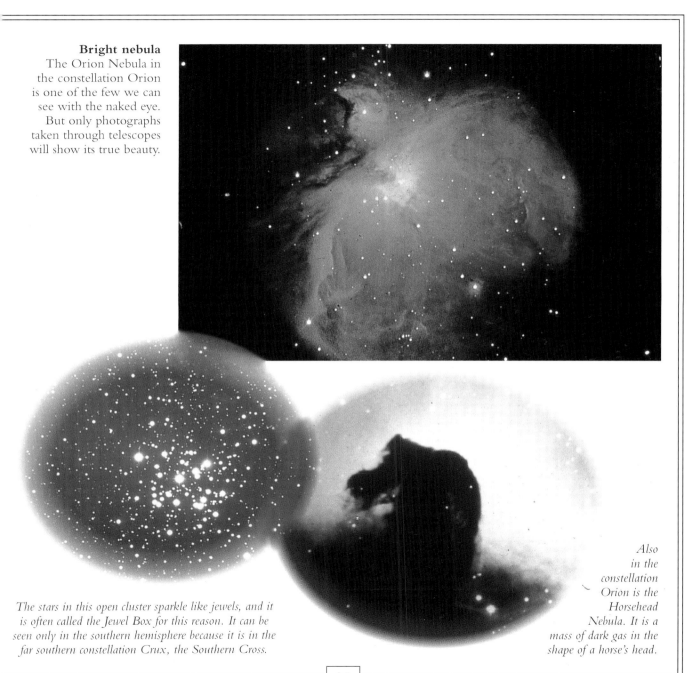

Bright nebula
The Orion Nebula in the constellation Orion is one of the few we can see with the naked eye. But only photographs taken through telescopes will show its true beauty.

The stars in this open cluster sparkle like jewels, and it is often called the Jewel Box for this reason. It can be seen only in the southern hemisphere because it is in the far southern constellation Crux, the Southern Cross.

Also in the constellation Orion is the Horsehead Nebula. It is a mass of dark gas in the shape of a horse's head.

GALAXIES OF STARS

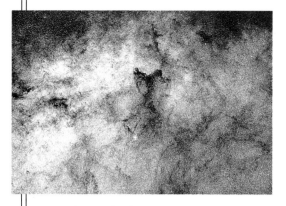

THE Sun and all the stars we see in the night sky belong to one great star system. The whole system is called a galaxy. Through very powerful telescopes, we can see many other galaxies like it. Between them there is empty space. Our own galaxy is called the Milky Way. This is also the name of the band of faint light that arches across the heavens, which we can see on a really dark night. In binoculars we can see that this band is made up of millions of stars, seemingly packed closely together.

A photograph of the Milky Way shows that it is made up of millions and millions of stars.

Milky Way

In our galaxy, most of the stars are grouped on curved or spiral arms coming out of the centre. If you could view it edge-on, it would look something like this (*above*). When you look at the Milky Way in the night sky, you are really looking at a cross-section, or slice, through the disc of our galaxy.

GALAXY TYPES

Our galaxy has a spiral shape. There are many other spiral galaxies like it in the heavens. Another kind of spiral galaxy is called a barred spiral. The arms come out of a bar through the bulge at the centre.

Spiral

A third common type is the elliptical galaxy. These may be round or oval in shape. They do not have any arms.

There are also irregular galaxies, which have no particular shape at all.

Barred spiral

Elliptical

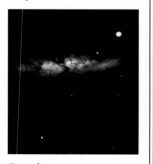

Irregular

Spiral galaxy

Our galaxy, the Milky Way, is classed as a spiral galaxy. At the centre is a great bulge of stars, and there are more stars farther out. They form long, curving (or spiral) arms. The Sun is found on one of these arms, quite a long way from the centre. The whole galaxy is rotating. If we could see it from a distance, it would look rather like a spinning Catherine wheel firework. Our galaxy is gigantic. It is made up of at least 100,000 million stars. It is so big that it would take a beam of light 100 million years to travel from one side to the other.

This galaxy is found in the constellation Andromeda. It is a spiral galaxy like our own. Our galaxy would look like this from a great distance.

THE BOUNDLESS UNIVERSE

WE know that the universe is made up of planets, moons, stars, nebulae and galaxies travelling through space. But most of the universe is just empty space. How big is the universe? No one really knows. Astronomers have already detected objects over 10,000 million light-years away, or 100,000 million million million kilometres away.

All galaxies are made up of millions of stars, which were born in the great clouds of gas and dust we call nebulae. This is the Lagoon Nebula in the constellation Sagittarius.

Earth

Solar system

Solar system

In our corner of the universe, the Earth is one of nine planets circling the Sun. The Sun is a star like the thousands we see in the night sky. All these stars form part of the Milky Way Galaxy. It is one of a small cluster of galaxies called the Local Group. About 30 galaxies make up the Local Group. The largest ones are spirals like the Milky Way and the Andromeda Galaxy.

Stars

Milky Way Galaxy

Local Group

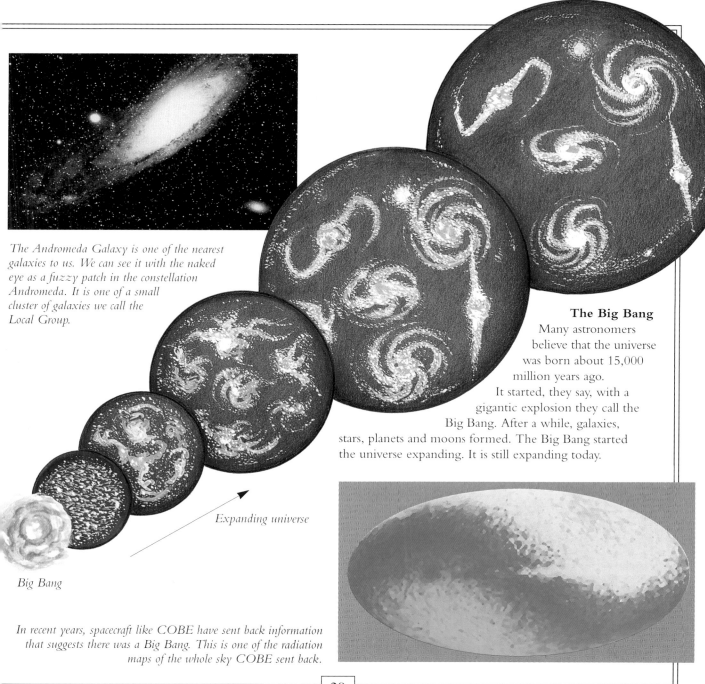

The Andromeda Galaxy is one of the nearest galaxies to us. We can see it with the naked eye as a fuzzy patch in the constellation Andromeda. It is one of a small cluster of galaxies we call the Local Group.

Expanding universe

Big Bang

In recent years, spacecraft like COBE have sent back information that suggests there was a Big Bang. This is one of the radiation maps of the whole sky COBE sent back.

The Big Bang
Many astronomers believe that the universe was born about 15,000 million years ago.
It started, they say, with a gigantic explosion they call the Big Bang. After a while, galaxies, stars, planets and moons formed. The Big Bang started the universe expanding. It is still expanding today.

EXPANDING THE UNIVERSE

WHEN astronomers study the galaxies, they find that they are all moving away from us and from one another at very high speeds. The universe is expanding. We can think of the universe as a balloon, being blown up bigger and bigger. If we blow up the balloon too much, it might burst. Could the universe end up doing that?

Have fun with balloons and discover the secrets of the universe!

MATERIALS

You will need: large balloons, balloon pump, stickers, string, scissors.

Make a universe

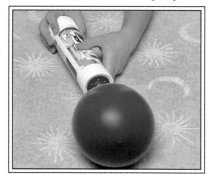

1 Partly blow up a round balloon. Puff into it gradually yourself, or use a balloon pump if you want to, which is easier.

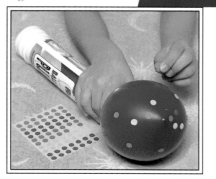

2 Stick spots on the partly blown-up balloon. Place them roughly the same distance apart. We can now think of this balloon now as the universe – the spots are the galaxies.

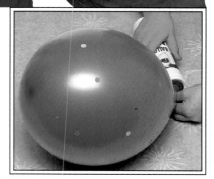

3 Carry on pumping. You see the balloon get bigger and the spots (galaxies) move farther apart – the universe is expanding!

Are there other universes?

We think we know what our universe is like. But is it the only universe? We used to think that the galaxy we live in was the only galaxy. Now we know of millions like it. So, some astronomers are wondering whether our universe is just one of many in a kind of super, multiple universe. Build a super, multiple universe yourself. Make a number of balloon universes like the one you made before. Tie them together with bits of string. You can think of the string as pathways between the universes. Maybe one day astronomers will find pathways like them.

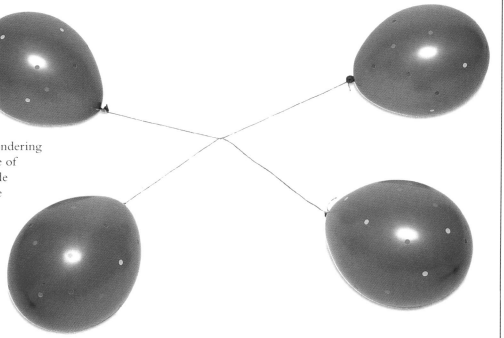

4 When the balloon is really big, take it off the pump. Hold it in your hands, pinching the neck.

5 Now let go of the neck so that the air rushes out. The balloon gets smaller and smaller, and the spots get closer together.

6 The balloon universe is shrinking and the galaxies are coming closer together. This is what astronomers think might happen to the real universe in the future.

OUR LOCAL STAR

The Sun glows fiery red just before it sets in the western sky. It does not look very big from the Earth. But it is huge. It could swallow more than a million Earths!

Seething surface

The surface of the Sun is a seething mass of boiling gas. In places, great fiery fountains leap thousands of kilometres high above the surface (*below*). They are called prominences. Smaller flares (*right*) spring up all over the place.

T HE most important body in our corner of the universe is the Sun. It is our local star. It appears to be much bigger and brighter than the other stars because it is much nearer. The Sun lies about 150 million kilometres away from the Earth. This is only a fraction of the distance to the next nearest star. The Sun is a lot bigger than the Earth, with a diameter of some 1,400,000 kilometres. Astronomers believe that the Sun has been shining for more than 5,000 million years and will continue to shine for another 5,000 million years.

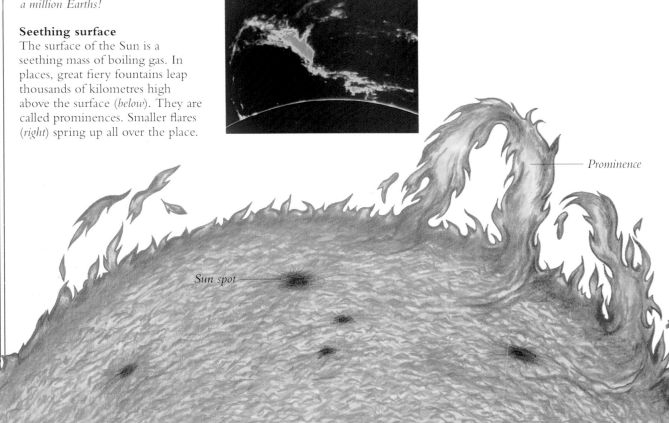

Prominence

Sun spot

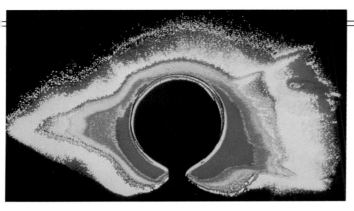

The Sun's crown

Astronauts in the Skylab space station carried out detailed studies of the Sun in 1973. They took many dramatic pictures. This one shows the corona (the outer atmosphere of the Sun).

If you have a telescope, you can view sunspots, projected onto a piece of paper, if you set it up in this way. You need the piece of card to shade the sheet of paper.

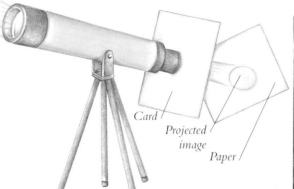

Card
Projected image
Paper

WARNING!

- **Never look at the Sun directly with your eyes or through binoculars or a telescope.**
- **The Sun is so bright that its light can blind you.**
- **The only safe way to view the Sun is by projection, as in the diagram above.**

Space station

NASA's Skylab space station in orbit in 1973. Three teams of astronauts spent 28, 59 and 84 days in turn carrying out observations and experiments.

Lights in space

Astronauts have also taken pictures of the aurora. This glow in the sky takes place at the North and South Poles when particles from the Sun collide with air particles in the Earth's atmosphere.

SUN AND EARTH

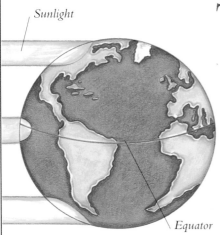

Sunlight

Equator

The heat in a sunbeam spreads over a greater area the farther you go away from the Equator.

T HE Sun keeps the Earth alive. Without the Sun's heat and light, the Earth would be a cold and lifeless lump of rock. It would be lifeless because living things need a reasonable temperature in which to live. Without sunlight plants could not grow, so there would be no food. Because the Earth is round, the Sun heats some parts of the Earth more than others. This gives rise to the different climates found on Earth. The hottest ones are around the Equator, and the coldest at the North and South Poles.

Rainbow colours
Sunlight is not golden, as you might think. It is made up of light of seven main colours. You see these colours in the rainbow. Raindrops split light into a rainbow, which has violet on the inside, then indigo, blue, green, yellow, orange and finally red on the outside.

Night and day
The Sun's light illuminates half of the Earth at any time. In this part, it is day. The part of the Earth away from the Sun is in darkness. In that part, it is night. But the Earth is spinning round on its axis. So everywhere on the Earth has day and night in turn.

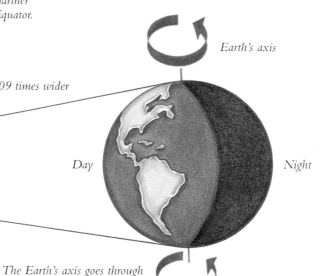

In fact, the Sun is nearly 109 times wider across than the Earth.

Earth's axis

Sun

Day

Night

The Earth's axis goes through the North and South Poles.

Seasons

The Earth's axis is tilted inspace. Each half of the world tilts more towards the Sun at some times of the year than at others. This makes each half hotter at some times than at others. Such changes in temperature mark what we call the seasons. The hottest time of the year is the season we call summer. The coldest is winter. Midway between winter and summer is spring. Midway between summer and winter is autumn.

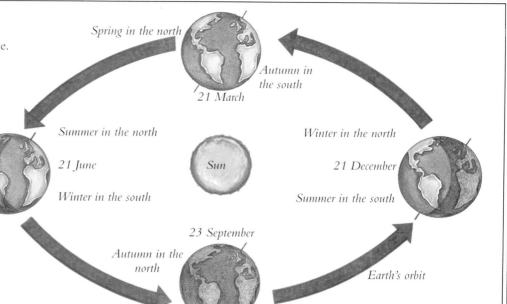

Spring in the north

21 March

Autumn in the south

Summer in the north

21 June

Winter in the south

Sun

Winter in the north

21 December

Summer in the south

23 September

Autumn in the north

Spring in the south

Earth's orbit

Sun rays

The Sun gives out not only light rays, but invisible rays as well. The ultraviolet rays it gives out are the ones that tan our bodies brown in the summer. But these rays can burn if we stay out in the Sun too long.

PHOTOSYNTHESIS

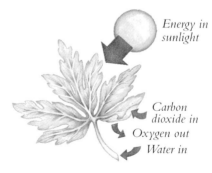

Energy in sunlight

Carbon dioxide in

Oxygen out

Water in

Plants use the energy in sunlight to make food in a process called photosynthesis. In the process, plants take in carbon dioxide from the air and water through their roots. These materials combine in the leaves to make sugar.

MAKING SUNDIALS

Thousands of years ago people used shadows to tell the time of day. They built simple shadow clocks. There was an upright piece called a gnomon, which cast shadows on a scale marking the time of day. Later, more accurate sundials were made, which had a sloping gnomon. There are many old sundials around still on walls and in gardens. Here, we show you how to make a simple sundial and also one you can carry around with you!

M A T E R I A L S

You will need: wooden pole, paint, paintbrush, hammer, string, scissors, teaspoon (to use as peg), pieces of coloured card, marker pens.

Make a garden sundial

1 Decorate the pole and bang it into the ground until it is firm. Watch your fingers! Tie one end of a piece of string to the top of the pole. Then peg the other end into the ground, a pole's length away.

2 The string becomes your gnomon. Every hour, place a card with the time marked on it where the shadow of the gnomon falls. Here, the girl is putting the 4 pm time card in place.

3 After you have done this all through one day, your sundial will be ready for use. On sunny days, you will be able to tell the time by looking at the shadows rather than at your watch.

Make a portable sundial

MATERIALS

You will need: piece of coloured card, pair of compasses, scissors, coloured pencils and paints, paintbrush, ruler, glue, flowerpot, wooden rod, magnetic compass.

Use the pair of compasses to draw a circle on the card and cut round it to leave a disc. Decorate the disc with 12 evenly spaced marks, for the hours of the day. Stick the disc on the upturned flowerpot. Push the rod through the middle of the disc. (You might want to clip the centre of the card first, to make it easier.) Now place the pot in the sunlight. Look at a magnetic compass and make a mark on the pot in the direction of north. Every hour during the day, mark where the shadow of the rod falls on the edge of the disc. Your portable sundial is now ready for use. Every time you use it, make sure that the north mark on the pot points north. Otherwise your sundial will be hours out!

Time for tea
This sundial is in the grounds of Herstmonceux Castle in southern England, the former site of the Royal Greenwich Observatory. The time is 16.00 hours, in other words, 4 pm.

THE MOON

The Moon measures 3,476 kilometres across. This is only about a quarter of the size of the Earth. Because it is so small, the Moon's gravity has a fairly weak pull.

WE know more about the Moon than about any other heavenly body because astronauts have landed on it and explored the surface. The Moon is our closest neighbour in space. It is the Earth's only satellite. It circles around the Earth at a distance of about 385,000 kilometres, and makes the journey about once a month. The Moon does not give out any light of its own. We see it because it reflects light from the Sun. The sunlight illuminates different parts of the Moon as the month goes by, making the Moon seem tc change shape. The Moon spins round slowly as it circles the Earth, so the same side always faces the Earth. The picture opposite shows what this nearside looks like. We only see it fully lit up once a month.

Astronaut Neil Armstrong planted the first footprint on the Moon on 20 July 1969.

Phases of the Moon

The shape of the Moon appears to change during the month. We call these changes in shape the Moon's phases. It takes the Moon 29½ days to change from a slim crescent to a full circle and back again.

TIDES

The Moon's pull causes the tides on Earth. When the Moon is overhead at the seaside, it pulls the water towards it, causing a high tide. Low tides occur when the Moon is elsewhere and has pulled the water away.

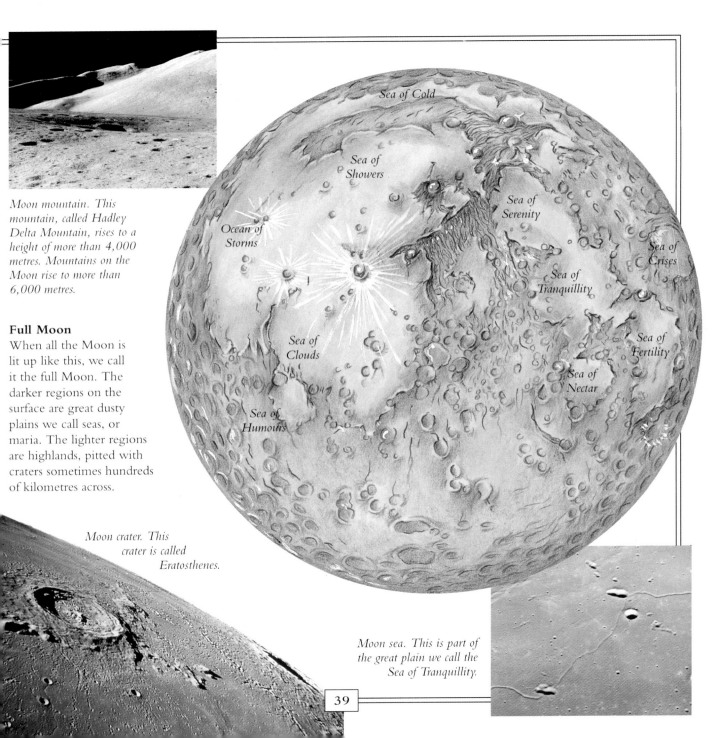

Moon mountain. This mountain, called Hadley Delta Mountain, rises to a height of more than 4,000 metres. Mountains on the Moon rise to more than 6,000 metres.

Full Moon

When all the Moon is lit up like this, we call it the full Moon. The darker regions on the surface are great dusty plains we call seas, or maria. The lighter regions are highlands, pitted with craters sometimes hundreds of kilometres across.

Sea of Cold

Sea of Showers

Sea of Serenity

Ocean of Storms

Sea of Crises

Sea of Tranquillity

Sea of Clouds

Sea of Fertility

Sea of Nectar

Sea of Humours

Moon crater. This crater is called Eratosthenes.

Moon sea. This is part of the great plain we call the Sea of Tranquillity.

MOON MOVEMENTS

Astronauts took this picture of the Moon when they flew around it in 1970.

T HE Moon travels around the Earth once a month and appears to change shape as it does so. You do not have to wait a month to see these changes in shape, or phases. You can carry out this project and watch the Moon go through its phases in a few minutes! All you need is a silvery ball, a torch, and a friend to help you.

M A T E R I A L S

You will need: football or beach ball, glue and brush, silver paper, torch.

Make your own Moon

1 Paint glue all over the ball. Rest it on a pot or something similar to keep it still.

2 Wrap up the ball in the silver paper, making sure it is as smooth as possible. You now have your Moon!

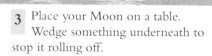

3 Place your Moon on a table. Wedge something underneath to stop it rolling off.

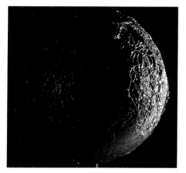

Crescent Moon

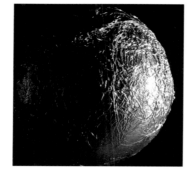

First Quarter phase

Full Moon

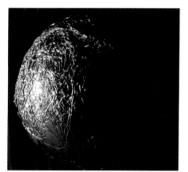

Last Quarter phase

Crescent Moon

Going through the phases

When you sit opposite your friend, the side of your Moon facing you will be in darkness. This is what happens once a month in the night sky when the opposite side of the Moon is lit up by the Sun. We cannot see the Moon, and we say it is a new Moon. As you move round the table, you will see more and more of your Moon lit up by the torch. All of it will be lit up when you look from behind your friend. When this kind of thing happens in the night sky, we call it a full Moon. As you carry on moving round, after your "full Moon" you will gradually see less and less of your Moon lit up. Your Moon will disappear when you are opposite your friend again. It will be another new Moon.

4 Get a friend to shine a torch with a strong beam on your Moon. Stand opposite and look at your Moon with the main lights out.

5 Gradually move round the table, still looking at your Moon, which is lit up one side by the torch.

SHADOWS IN SPACE

THE Moon circles around the Earth as the Earth circles around the Sun. Once or twice a year, the Moon comes between the Sun and the Earth. It may completely or partly block out the light from the Sun, leaving the Earth in shadow. We call this an eclipse of the Sun, or a solar eclipse. Also, at times, the Earth comes between the Sun and the Moon. It blots out the light from the Sun and leaves the Moon in shadow. We call this an eclipse of the Moon, or a lunar eclipse.

Orbit of Moon around the Earth

Sun

Moon

Umbra

Earth

Total eclipse of Sun seen here

Solar eclipse
Eclipses of the Sun occur when the Moon casts a shadow on the Earth. A complete shadow, called an umbra, can be seen only over a small area. There, a total eclipse takes place. A part shadow, called a penumbra, can be seen over a much bigger area. There, a partial eclipse takes place.

Lunar eclipse
Eclipses of the Moon occur when the Moon passes into the shadow cast by the Earth. The Moon can stay in eclipse for a number of hours, because the Earth casts a big shadow in space. An eclipse of the Sun lasts only a few minutes at most, because the Moon casts such a small shadow.

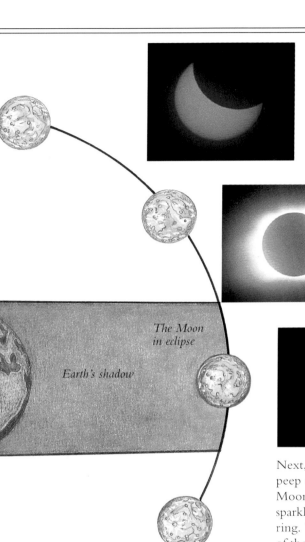

Eclipse of the Sun

An eclipse of the Sun starts when the Moon begins to move across the face of the Sun. Gradually, the Moon covers more and more of the Sun and daylight turns into twilight.

Soon the Moon covers the Sun completely and it suddenly gets dark. Then we see the white halo (corona) around the dark Moon.

The Moon in eclipse

Earth's shadow

Next, the Sun begins to peep over the edge of the Moon. It looks rather like a sparkling diamond in a ring. That is why this stage of the eclipse is called the diamond ring.

Seconds later, the Moon moves on and uncovers more of the Sun. Daylight returns once more.

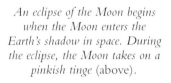

An eclipse of the Moon begins when the Moon enters the Earth's shadow in space. During the eclipse, the Moon takes on a pinkish tinge (above).

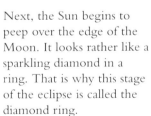

The sky does not get completely dark during a solar eclipse. There is light in the distance around the horizon. .

THE SUN'S FAMILY

THE Earth and the Sun travel through space together. The Earth is one of a family of bodies that circle around the Sun in space. These bodies are called the planets. Many of the planets have smaller bodies, called moons, circling around them. All these bodies form part of the Sun's family, which is called the solar system. As well as the planets, other bodies circle around the Sun. Some are swarms of small bodies we call asteroids, and others are icy lumps we call comets. The whole solar system of planets, moons, asteroids and comets is held together by the Sun's enormous pull (gravity).

Saturn

Jupiter

Mercury   Venus   Earth   Mars

Sun

The planets
The nine planets lie at different distances from the Sun. Nearest to the Sun is Mercury, farthest away is Pluto. The planets vary widely in size. The four planets closest to the Sun are much smaller than the next four, which we call the giant planets.

The Sun
The Sun lies at the heart of the solar system. It is not the same kind of body as the planets. It is a star, a great ball of glowing gas that gives out enormous energy as heat and light.

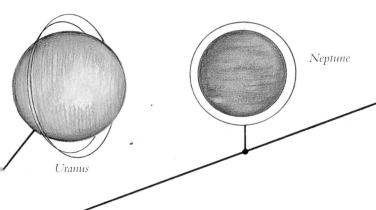

This diagram shows roughly to scale how far apart the planets are. The sizes of the planets are not drawn to scale.

Uranus

Neptune

Pluto

Tiny Pluto

Pluto is the most distant and by far the smallest planet. Even smaller bodies are found much farther away still.

Huge planets

The giant planets are truly gigantic and are quite unlike the Earth. They are made up mainly of gas, while the Earth is made up mainly of rock.

It was not until the 1500s that astronomers such as Copernicus began to realise that the Earth and the planets circle around the Sun.

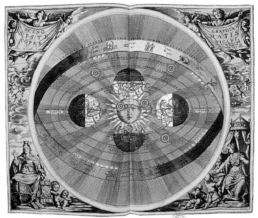

FACTBOX

• The Sun is the only body in the solar system that gives out light. The other bodies shine because they reflect the Sun's light.

• Jupiter weighs more than all the other planets put together.

• Saturn is so light that if you could put it in water, it would float.

• Mercury takes only 88 days to circle around the Sun. Pluto takes nearly 250 years.

Ancient astronomers thought that the Earth was the centre of the universe. It seemed to them that the Sun, the Moon, the planets and the stars circled around the Earth.

SCALING THE SOLAR SYSTEM

At the centre of the solar system, the Sun sends rays of heat and light towards the planets.

Mercury, Venus, Earth and Mars lie quite close to the Sun. Mercury and Venus are so close that they are baking hot. Earth is not too hot and not too cold. Living things like it here! They would not like Mars – it is too cold.

THE planets are spread out over vast distances in space. It is difficult on two pages of a book to give a true impression of the scale of the solar system. But this project should help. The idea is for you and your friends to take the place of the planets and sit in a line at different distances from a friend who is the Sun. The people playing Mercury, Venus, Earth and Mars sit close together and close to the Sun. Those playing the other planets sit much farther apart. Use your imagination and cutting, painting and pasting skills to make hats showing which planet you are. This is what would happen if we used the same scale for the distances for Jupiter and the other planets as we do on this page for all the planets, from Mercury to Mars. Jupiter would appear in the middle of page 48, Saturn on page 50, Uranus on page 54, Neptune on page 59, and we could not get Pluto in the book at all!

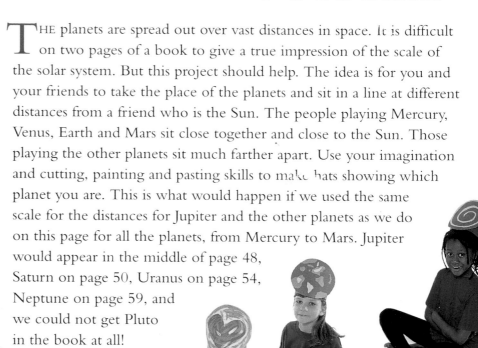

M A T E R I A L S

You will need: coloured paper, marker pens, coloured pencils, scissors, ruler, coloured tape, stick-on dots and stars.

Four giants

The four planets close to the Sun are tiny compared with the next four planets. Jupiter, Saturn, Uranus and Neptune are very much bigger. They are also very much farther apart from one another.

Jupiter is the biggest planet of them all. If it had been much bigger when it formed, it might have become a star, not a planet.

Saturn is the most beautiful of the planets because of the shining rings that surround it.

Uranus and its twin, Neptune, have rings round them, but we cannot see them from Earth. Here, Neptune is shown walking because it is a lot farther away.

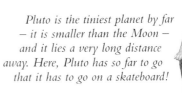

Pluto is the tiniest planet by far – it is smaller than the Moon – and it lies a very long distance away. Here, Pluto has so far to go that it has to go on a skateboard!

Mercury

Venus

Earth

Mars

Jupiter

Saturn

Uranus

Neptune

Pluto

MERCURY, VENUS AND EARTH

MERCURY, Venus and Earth are the three planets closest to the Sun. Mercury and Venus are made up of rock like the Earth and have a similar structure. But they are unlike the Earth in other ways. Mercury has a very hot, sun-baked surface and has no air, or atmosphere, around it. Venus is nearly the same size as the Earth and has an atmosphere. But this is made up of carbon dioxide and is very thick. Its pressure would crush human beings. The atmosphere acts like a greenhouse and causes the planet to heat up to the temperature of a very hot oven.

Earth

Mercury

Mercury
Mercury looks much like the Moon because it is covered with many thousands of craters. The space probe Mariner 10 sent back this picture (*above*) when it visited the planet in 1974.

This picture from Mariner 10 shows a close-up of Mercury's cratered surface (right). The craters measure up to 50 kilometres across.

Small planet
Compared with the Earth, Mercury is tiny. It is the second smallest planet, after Pluto. But while Pluto is very cold, Mercury is very hot. In places, temperatures can rise to more than 450 degrees Celsius.

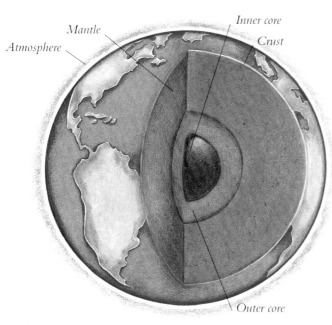

Atmosphere
Mantle
Inner core
Crust
Outer core

Earth from space
Earth looks beautiful from space. This picture was taken by the Apollo astronauts. It shows most of Africa, Arabia and Asia. Europe is mostly under cloud.

Venus from space
We cannot see the surface of Venus from the Earth. This is because thick clouds fill the atmosphere. The space probe Mariner 10 took this photograph of Venus in 1974, showing the pattern of swirling clouds.

Hard and soft Earth

The Earth is made up mainly of rock. On the outside is hard rock, forming a thin layer we call the crust. Underneath is a thick layer of warm softer rock, which makes up the mantle. The inner and outer cores are made up mainly of iron.

Surface of Venus

We now know what the surface of Venus is like. Space probes have used radar beams to "look" through the clouds. The surface is covered with many craters. There are just a few highland areas.

FACTBOX

• The temperatures on the planets Mercury and Venus are high enough to melt lead and other metals.

• The clouds in Venus's atmosphere are made up of sulphuric acid.

• The crust of the Earth is only about 8 kilometres thick in places.

• Oceans cover more than two-thirds of the Earth's surface.

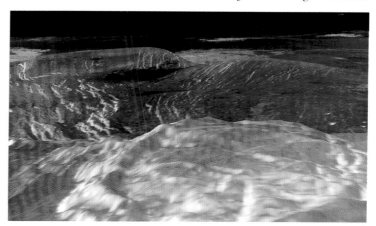

ALL FALL DOWN

WHEN you drop something, it falls. Something must therefore be pulling it down. That something is the Earth. We call the Earth's pull gravity. The Sun and all other planets have gravity too. The Sun's gravity pulls at all the planets and keeps them in place in the solar system. But back on Earth, if you drop a light thing and a heavy thing, which one hits the ground first? Common sense tells us that it must be the heavy one. But is this true? Carry out this experiment and find out. An Italian scientist named Galileo (1564–1642) is supposed to have carried out a similar experiment by dropping cannonballs from the top of the Leaning Tower of Pisa.

Hundreds of kilometres above the Earth, an astronaut floats in space. We say he is weightless, but gravity is still tugging at his body.

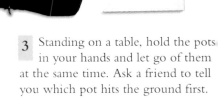

Testing gravity

1 Paint the yoghurt pots a suitable colour – perhaps one grey (= metal = heavy), the other blue (= sky = air = light).

2 Fill the grey (= heavy) pot with sand. Leave the blue (= light) one empty. Cover them both with kitchen foil and tape them firmly.

3 Standing on a table, hold the pots in your hands and let go of them at the same time. Ask a friend to tell you which pot hits the ground first.

You will need: yoghurt pots, paint, paintbrush, sand, kitchen foil, scissors, sticky tape, small orange, large balloon.

4 Here are the two pots falling. They start together. Half-way down they are neck and neck.

5 Then thud, they hit the ground – at the same time.

Breaking the law?
From the experiment with the yoghurt pots, we can state a scientific law: that falling bodies fall to Earth at the same rate. Now, carry out the same experiment using a small orange and a large balloon. Do they both hit the ground at the same time? If they do not, can you think why they do not?

MARS AND MINI-PLANETS

ARS is another rocky planet like the Earth. But it is much smaller and has hardly any atmosphere. Temperatures on Mars do not often rise above freezing point, even in the Martian summer. People used to think that intelligent beings lived on Mars, but we know now that this is not possible. Several space probes, such as Viking, have visited the planet, but they have found no signs of life. They have, however, revealed some spectacular features. These include a huge Martian "Grand Canyon" and ancient volcanoes bigger than any that have been found on Earth.

The surface of Mars is a rusty brown colour. The flat plains are covered with a sandy kind of soil and are littered with rocks.

Mars

Earth

Mars is a little over half as wide across as the Earth.

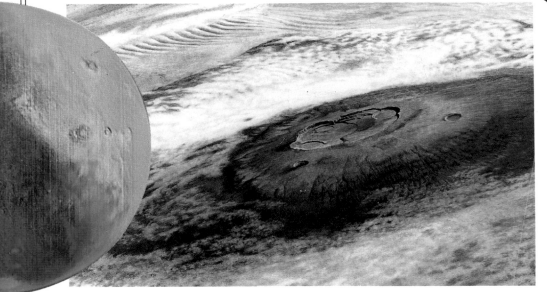

Volcanic Mars
Several huge ancient volcanoes have been found on Mars. They can be seen in photographs taken from space. They appear as circles in the false-colour photograph taken by a Viking probe *(far left)*. The biggest volcano *(left)* is known as Mount Olympus. It towers to a height of 25 kilometres.

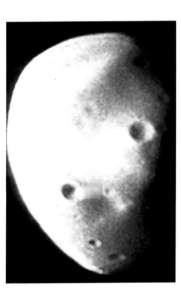

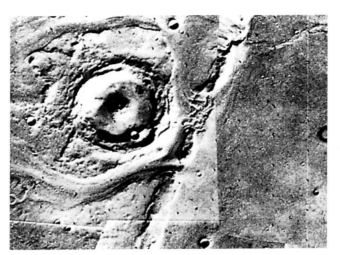

This is one of the two moons of Mars, called Deimos. It measures about 20 kilometres across.

The two Viking space probes were sent to map the surface of Mars, beginning in 1976. They each split into two parts. One went into orbit and the other landed. The orbiters showed areas covered with craters and canyons (above). The picture (right) shows part of one of the landers.

Mini-planets

A swarm of rocky bodies is found between the orbits of Mars and Jupiter. We call them asteroids. Most of them orbit the Sun in a broad band we call the asteroid belt. A few wander out of the belt, some quite close to the Earth. Even the largest asteroid, Ceres, is only about a third of the size of our Moon. Its diameter is about 1,000 kilometres.

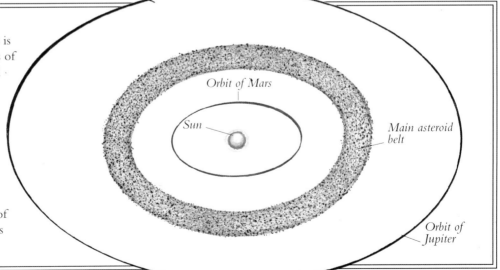

Orbit of Mars

Sun

Main asteroid belt

Orbit of Jupiter

JUPITER THE GIANT

JUPITER is by far the biggest planet. To compare it with Earth, imagine Jupiter as a tennis ball and Earth as a pea. Jupiter is one of the so-called giant planets, which are made up in a different way from Earth. Jupiter has a tiny ball of rock at the centre. Above this come layers of hydrogen in different forms – as a kind of metal, as liquid and as gas in the atmosphere. When we look at Jupiter in telescopes, we see coloured bands in the atmosphere. They are clouds that have been drawn out into bands as the planet spins round rapidly.

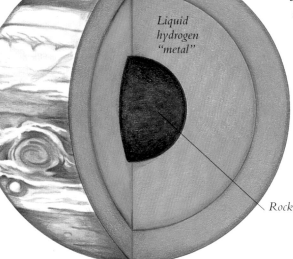

Earth

Hydrogen gas
atmosphere

Liquid
hydrogen

Liquid
hydrogen
"metal"

Rock

Jupiter measures more than 140,000 kilometres across. It is made up mainly of hydrogen in the form of a gas and a liquid.

Colourful Jupiter
Jupiter is one of the most colourful planets. Among its many moons is Europa *(right)*. The colourful bands you see in Jupiter's atmosphere are fast-moving clouds. The spots you can see are furious storms.

Big moons

Ganymede and Io are two of Jupiter's four big moons. Here, they are compared in size with the Earth's Moon. But they are different from the Moon. They contain a lot of ice as well as rock.

Ganymede has a diameter of nearly 5,300 kilometres. It is the biggest moon in the solar system.

Spot on Jupiter

The most famous feature of Jupiter is the Great Red Spot. It is a huge storm of furiously whirling winds. This picture has been printed in false colours to show the patterns of clouds swirling about.

Earth's Moon

Io is brightly coloured because it is covered with sulphur. The sulphur comes from volcanoes.

FACTBOX

• Jupiter has no solid surface. It is covered with a deep ocean of liquid hydrogen.

• A day on Jupiter is less than 10 hours long.

• Jupiter has at least 16 moons. The biggest, Ganymede, is larger than the planet Mercury.

• Jupiter has a ring around it, but it is too faint to be seen from the Earth.

One of Jupiter's moons

In close-up photographs, Callisto has a fascinating surface. There are dark regions and light ones with patterns of grooves. Tiny craters are everywhere, many ringed with ice.

MORE GIANTS

SATURN, Uranus and Neptune are the three other giant planets that are made up largely of gases. All three have systems of rings around them, but only Saturn's rings can be easily seen from Earth. They are one of the wonders of the solar system. Like Jupiter, these other giants have many moons – Saturn at least 22, Uranus at least 15 and Neptune at least eight. Uranus and Neptune cannot be seen with the naked eye from Earth. Uranus was not discovered until 1781 and Neptune not until 1846. The ninth planet, Pluto, was not discovered until 1930. But it is not a giant. It is a tiny body much smaller than Earth's Moon. Strangely, it has a moon that is half its size, which is relatively big for a moon.

The many ringlets in Saturn's rings show up in this false-colour picture. The different colours show that the ringlets are made up of particles of different sizes.

This is Titan, Saturn's largest moon. It is the only moon we know that has a thick atmosphere.

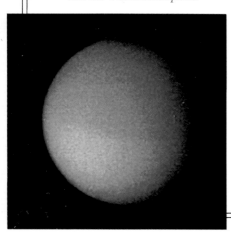

Bright rings
The Voyager 2 space probe took this beautiful picture of Saturn from a distance of about 40 million kilometres. Two bright rings can be seen, separated by a gap. Saturn has at least 22 moons. You can see two of them in the picture. One of them is casting a shadow on the planet.

Distant Uranus

Uranus lies so far away that it takes 84 years to circle around the Sun. Like all the other planets, Uranus spins round as it travels in its orbit. But unlike all the other planets, Uranus spins on its side as it travels. The other planets spin round in a more or less upright position, like a top, as they travel along their orbits.

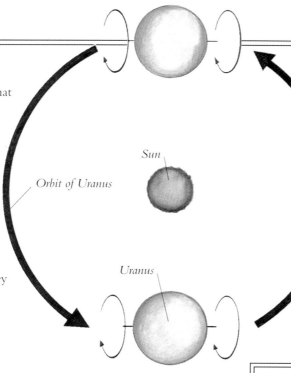

Sun

Orbit of Uranus

Uranus

Triton, Neptune's largest moon, has a surface covered in snow and ice. Here and there, geysers shoot cold gas high above the surface.

Blue Uranus

Uranus has a thick atmosphere with a bluish colour. This covers a deep ocean of water and gases. We cannot see any clouds or storms in the atmosphere in the way that we can see them on Jupiter and Saturn.

Blue Neptune

Neptune, Uranus's twin, is another blue planet. But, unlike Uranus, it has some interesting features. There are patches of white cloud and dark oval regions. The biggest, shown here, is called the Great Dark Spot.

TINY PLUTO

Pluto

Earth

The ninth planet in the solar system, Pluto, has a diameter of about 2,300 kilometres. It is even smaller than the Moon. We know little about Pluto. We cannot see it very well with telescopes because it is so small and so far away. Space probes have not visited it yet. But it is almost certainly made up of ice, frozen gases and a little rock.

METEORS AND COMETS

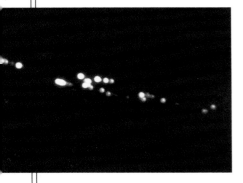

This unusual photograph shows a meteorite breaking up as it plunges through the atmosphere. The small pieces will burn to ash, but the bigger ones might reach the ground.

Dinosaur bones

Some scientists believe that the dinosaurs died out when a huge meteorite struck the Earth. They think the dust it kicked up blotted out the Sun, and the plants that the dinosaurs lived on died.

SOMETIMES when you are stargazing, you see a streak of light in the sky that looks like a star falling down. A falling star, or a shooting star, is actually a meteor. A meteor is a bit of rock from outer space that burns up as it travels through the atmosphere. If it is big enough, it might reach the ground. Then we call it a meteorite. Large meteorites can make big craters. We can still see a few large meteorite craters on the Earth, and there are many on the Moon and on other bodies in the solar system. Most of the bits of rock that cause meteors have come from passing comets. Comets are great lumps of icy rock that appear in our skies from time to time. They gradually break up into dust and gas and glow in the sunlight. Some break up over thousands of years. Bright comets are a magnificent spectacle.

Meteorites helped shape Saturn's moon Enceladus.

Hole in the desert

The Arizona Meteor Crater is located in the Arizona Desert, USA. A huge meteorite made the crater when it fell to Earth about 25,000 years ago. The crater measures nearly 1,300 metres across and 175 metres deep.

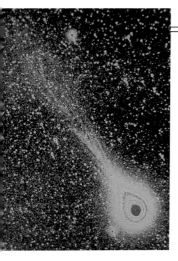

This false-colour picture of a comet shows differences in brightness. The region in the centre of the comet's head is brightest (red). The tail (blue) is quite faint.

Returning comet

A comet appeared at the time of the Battle of Hastings in 1066. It was recorded on the Bayeux Tapestry. Comets were thought to bring bad luck. So it proved for the English King Harold, who was killed. The comet that appeared in 1066 returns to our skies about every 76 years. It is now called Halley's Comet, after Edmond Halley, who was the first to realize it was a regular visitor.

Halley's comet last appeared in Earth's skies in 1986. It will not be seen again until 2062.

Comet's tail

Comets grow a tail when they get near the Sun. The tail is made up of gas and dust, which reflect sunlight. The "pressure" of particles coming from the Sun pushes the gas and dust away from the comet's head to form a tail. Notice that the tail of the comet always points away from the Sun.

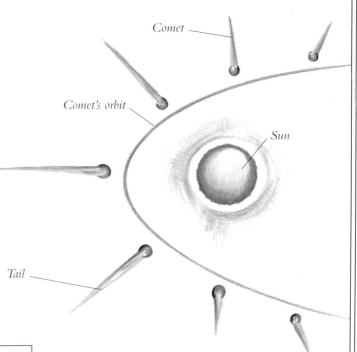

Comet

Comet's orbit

Sun

Tail

ASTRONOMERS AT WORK

ASTRONOMERS study the stars with their eyes, with binoculars, telescopes, radio receivers, electronic sensors, and much other equipment besides. They work in places called observatories. Most observatories are located high up in a dry climate. There, they are above the thickest and dirtiest part of the atmosphere. In a dry climate there is less moisture in the air and less chance of cloud. Telescopes are the main instruments astronomers use. The Italian astronomer Galileo first studied the heavens through a telescope in about 1609. He used a telescope in which glass lenses gathered and focused the light. This kind of telescope is called a refractor. But most astronomers today use telescopes in which mirrors gather and focus the light. These are called reflectors. Some have mirrors up to six metres across.

An amateur astronomer with a useful sized reflector for serious stargazing. Mirrors gather and focus the light and reflect an image into the eyepiece for viewing.

Top of the world

Kitt Peak Observatory (*above*) is one of the world's finest laboratories. It occupies a mountain site in the Arizona Desert, USA. The domes house large reflecting telescopes. The latest telescopes (*left*) have a skeleton frame for lightness.

Powerful telescope

The Hubble Space Telescope *(right)* is the most powerful light telescope put into space. The pictures it sends back show much more detail than pictures taken from big telescopes on the ground.

The Hubble Space Telescope took this picture of the heart of a distant galaxy, with gas clouds and many globular clusters. Telescopes on the ground show the galaxy as a white blob.

Pictures from space

Astronomers use their big telescopes as cameras. They expose the film for long periods, so that the faint light from distant stars and galaxies builds up to give a brighter image *(above)*.

Satellites

Astronomers use satellites to carry instruments into space. The satellite IRAS looked at the heavens using invisible infrared light. It spotted great clouds of gas among the stars in the constellation Orion *(left)*. The star marked alpha (α) in the picture is one of the biggest stars we know, the supergiant Betelgeuse.

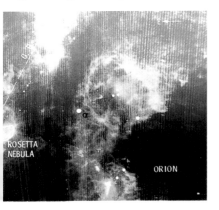

ROSETTA NEBULA

ORION

A radio picture of a distant galaxy (right). *It was made by using a computer to process the radio waves that the galaxy gives out.*

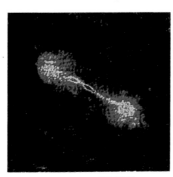

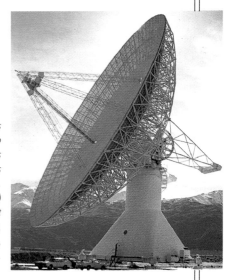

Radio telescopes collect the radio waves stars and galaxies give out. This one (right) is located at Owens Valley, California, USA.

MAKING A TELESCOPE

Iɴ their observatories, astronomers look at the night sky with reflectors – telescopes with mirrors. But these are difficult to make. Here we show you how to make a refractor – a telescope with glass lenses. You cannot use any lenses. You need to buy special ones from a hobby shop. When you buy the lenses for the telescope, ask for one lens with a long focal length (about 30 centimetres) for the objective lens, and one with a short focal length (about 5 centimetres) for the eyepiece.

An old astronomer explains to a young one how his reflector works.

M A T E R I A L S

You will need: lenses, cardboard tube, reusable adhesive, stiff black paper, sticky tape, scissors, stickers.

An astronomer looks through a large refractor. This one has a main lens 70 centimetres across.

Make your own refractor

1 Fix the objective lens into one end of the cardboard tube with reusable adhesive.

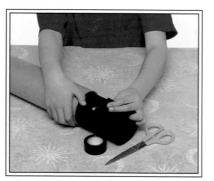

2 Roll the black paper into a tube shape so that it fits inside the other end of the cardboard tube.

3 Adjust the width of the tube so that it can take the eyepiece lens. Then fix the lens with tape.

Objective and eyepiece

This diagram shows you how a refractor is made up. The end lens of the telescope (the objective lens) gathers the light from the stars and forms an image, or picture. You view the image with a lens near the eye (the eyepiece lens).

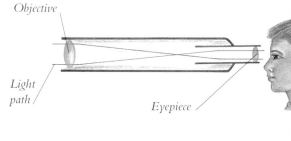

Objective

Light path

Eyepiece

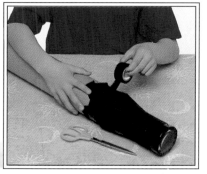

4 If there is a gap between the two tubes, make a sleeve with some more black paper.

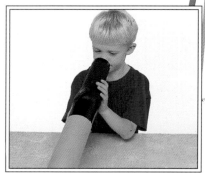

5 Look at a distant object with your telescope. Slide the eyepiece tube in or out until you see a sharp image. If necessary, adjust the lengths of the telescope tubes.

6 Decorate the tube if you want to. When your telescope is ready, mount it on a tripod and look up at the stars. You can make a tripod out of broom handles (see page 7).

INDEX

PICTURE CREDITS
b=bottom, t=top, c=centre,
l=left, r=right
Spacecharts/Royal
Astronomical Society Library:
page 41. Spacecharts: pages
5 tl, tr; 11tr; 22 tl; 24bl; 25;
26 t, cl, cr, bl, br; 28tr; 29 tr,
br; 38 tr, bl, cb; 39 tl, tr; 40tl;
43 tr, tl; 48 tl, bc; 49rb; 50tl;
52 tl, bl; 53 tl, tr; 54rb; 55 tr,
bl; 56 tl, bl; 57 tr, c, bl; 58tl;
59 tl,tr,cl; 60 tl, cr, bl; 61 tr,
tl, cr, bl, cb, br.
Robin Kerrod: pages 5 tl, br;
8bl; 10tr; 11bl; 34; 35; 43.
NASA: page 58cr.
Natural History Museum:
page 58bl.